Learn your times tables

Book 1

2x 5x 10x

Duncan Grime

Acknowledgements:

Author: Duncan Grime

Series Editor: Peter Sumner
Cover and Page Design: Kathryn Webster

The right of Duncan Grime to be identified as the author of this publication has been asserted by him in accordance with the Copyright, Designs and Patents Act 1998.

HeadStart Primary Ltd,
Elker Lane,
Clitheroe,
BB7 9HZ

T. 01200 423405
E. info@headstartprimary.com
www.headstartprimary.com

Published by HeadStart Primary Ltd 2018 © **HeadStart Primary Ltd 2018**

A record for this book is available from the British Library -
ISBN: 978-1-908767-22-6

HeadStart Primary : Learn your times tables
Book 1 (2, 5 and 10 times tables)

Guidance Notes

Introduction - about the book

This book has been written by a practising teacher. Its purpose is clear; it is designed to help children develop a thorough recall of the times tables. A sound understanding of all the multiplication tables is vital if children are to become competent and confident mathematicians. Mastery of this knowledge is a major component in the assembly of basic number skills.

The learning has been structured so that children can build their confidence quickly, each step providing a solid foundation for the next one. This is much more than just a times tables practice book. It uses tried and tested visual and auditory techniques, whilst encouraging oral participation that reinforces the learning process.

Format - the structure of the book and audio CD

Each multiplication table is split into manageable sections so that a child can progress at a pace which is comfortable for them. The sections are intended to be learnt separately and then re-connected in stages until all the times table can be chanted and recalled fluently.

The sections of each book are complemented by the tracks on the audio CD. The spoken word on the CD is intended to help the learner establish a rhythm when chanting the tables and answering questions. This rhythm will consolidate the learning taking place, embedding the table firmly in the child's repertoire. The pace of the spoken word is deliberately steady to build up clear understanding at every stage. Once a table is learnt, a quickening of pace may be appropriate to cement the effect of the rhythm.

Each track on the CD or unit in the book can be repeated as many times as necessary until the child is confident enough to move on to the next section. Learning will build incrementally until the whole times table can be chanted and recalled with confidence.

Further guidance - notes on using the book and CDs

- For the 2, 5 and 10 times tables, Tabby the Table Dragon directs the child, giving tips and advice on each page. Tabby also indicates when a page links to a track on the audio CD.

- Learning can be reinforced by colouring or finger tracing over the larger numbers on several of the pages. This could be an activity carried out whilst listening to tracks on the audio CD.

- Several pages have an empty 'minutes' circle at the top of the page. This can be used to provide a fitting level of challenge depending on the ability of the learner. Similarly, at the foot of each page is a 'Score and Time' record, which can also be used to provide additional incentive or challenge.

- Children can be encouraged to circle or colour one of the three faces towards the bottom left of each page. In this way, progress and growing confidence can be tracked.

- The extension work on Tracks 11,12 and 13 of the audio CD are there to test the knowledge of children who have a sound grasp of the whole table. These could be used as games where various challenges are set.

- Some of the games and activities at the end of each table may need the help of an adult to organise and explain. The activities will be accessible to most children but they incorporate extra challenge for more able learners. It is intended that these pages will reinforce the learning that has taken place as well as letting children have fun with their newly acquired knowledge.

- The CD-ROM containing the PDF of the book can be used on an interactive whiteboard or for printing.

The

times table

CONTENTS: 2 times table

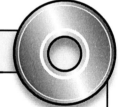

Hello! I'm Tabby the Table Dragon. I am going to help you learn your two times table.

Listen to Track 1 on the CD. Take note of the rhythm and join in when you are ready. Then try to put in the answers on Track 2.

1 x 2 = 2

2 x 2 = 4

3 x 2 = 6

4 x 2 = 8

Name ....

Hello! Tabby the Table Dragon here! Can you fill in the spaces with the correct numbers?

1
a) 1 x 2 = ☐
b) 2 x 2 = ☐
c) 3 x 2 = ☐
d) 4 x 2 = ☐

2
a) 1 x 2 = ☐
b) 2 x 2 = ☐
c) 3 x 2 = ☐
d) 4 x 2 = ☐

3
a) ☐ x 2 = 2
b) ☐ x 2 = 4
c) ☐ x 2 = 6
d) ☐ x 2 = 8

4
a) ☐ x 2 = 2
b) 2 x ☐ = 4
c) ☐ x 2 = 6
d) 4 x 2 = ☐

How did you do?

Score................. Time.................

© Copyright HeadStart Primary Ltd

2

Name ....

Now you are going to get a score. See how many you can get right in the time given.

◯ minutes!

1
a	3	x	2	=	☐
b	1	x	2	=	☐
c	4	x	2	=	☐
d	2	x	2	=	☐
e	1	x	2	=	☐
f	4	x	2	=	☐
g	3	x	2	=	☐
h	2	x	2	=	☐

2
a	1	x	2	=	☐
b	4	x	2	=	☐
c	2	x	2	=	☐
d	3	x	2	=	☐
e	4	x	2	=	☐
f	1	x	2	=	☐
g	3	x	2	=	☐
h	2	x	2	=	☐

3
a	4	x	2	=	☐
b	1	x	2	=	☐
c	3	x	2	=	☐
d	2	x	2	=	☐
e	1	x	2	=	☐
f	3	x	2	=	☐
g	2	x	2	=	☐
h	4	x	2	=	☐

4
a	2	x	2	=	☐
b	4	x	2	=	☐
c	1	x	2	=	☐
d	3	x	2	=	☐
e	4	x	2	=	☐
f	2	x	2	=	☐
g	3	x	2	=	☐
h	1	x	2	=	☐

How did you do?

Score.................. Time..................

3

Name ....

On this page draw lines to join up the two parts of the times table. One has been done for you.

1
a	3	x	2	8
b	4	x	2	4
c	1	x	2	6
d	2	x	2	2

2
a	2	x	2	2
b	1	x	2	6
c	4	x	2	4
d	3	x	2	8

3

3 x 2   1 x 2   6   4

4 x 2   2 x 2   2   8

4

8   3 x 2   6   2 x 2

1 x 2   4   4 x 2   2

How did you do?   Score................. Time.................

4

Name ....

See if you can work out the answers on Spikey the Spider's legs.

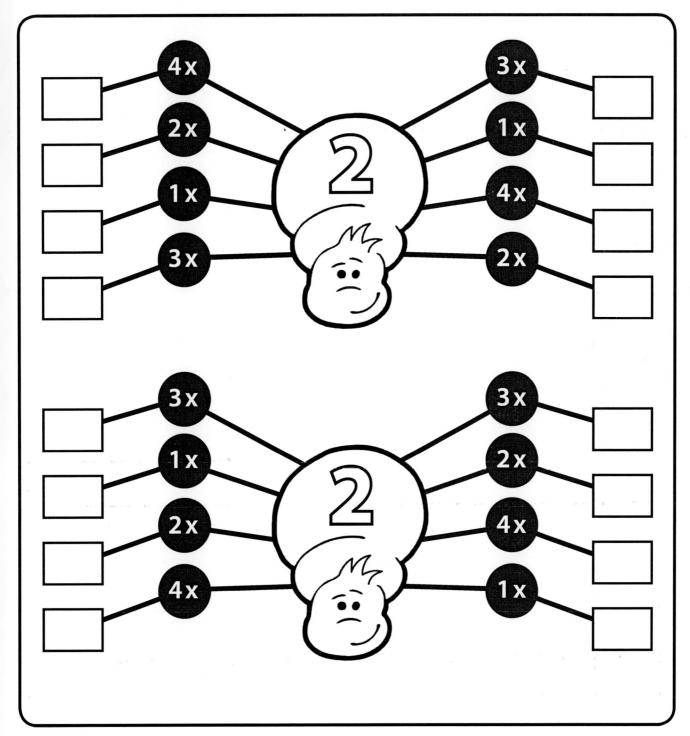

How did you do?

Score................. Time.................

Name ....

Tabby here. Well done! Let's move on to the next part.

Listen to Track 3 on the CD and join in when you are ready. Then try and put the answers in on Track 4.

5 x 2 = 10

6 x 2 = 12

7 x 2 = 14

8 x 2 = 16

Name ....

Hi. Try to fill in the spaces with the correct numbers.

1
a) 5 x 2 = ☐
b) 6 x 2 = ☐
c) 7 x 2 = ☐
d) 8 x 2 = ☐

2
a) 5 x 2 = ☐
b) 6 x 2 = ☐
c) 7 x 2 = ☐
d) 8 x 2 = ☐

3
a) ☐ x 2 = 10
b) ☐ x 2 = 12
c) ☐ x 2 = 14
d) ☐ x 2 = 16

4
a) ☐ x 2 = 10
b) 6 x ☐ = 12
c) ☐ x 2 = 14
d) 8 x 2 = ☐

How did you do?

Score................. Time.................

( ) minutes!

This time, see if you can get them all right in the time given.

1
a	7 x 2 =	
b	5 x 2 =	
c	8 x 2 =	
d	6 x 2 =	
e	5 x 2 =	
f	8 x 2 =	
g	7 x 2 =	
h	6 x 2 =	

2
a	5 x 2 =	
b	8 x 2 =	
c	6 x 2 =	
d	7 x 2 =	
e	8 x 2 =	
f	5 x 2 =	
g	7 x 2 =	
h	6 x 2 =	

3
a	8 x 2 =	
b	5 x 2 =	
c	7 x 2 =	
d	6 x 2 =	
e	5 x 2 =	
f	7 x 2 =	
g	6 x 2 =	
h	8 x 2 =	

4
a	6 x 2 =	
b	8 x 2 =	
c	5 x 2 =	
d	7 x 2 =	
e	8 x 2 =	
f	6 x 2 =	
g	7 x 2 =	
h	5 x 2 =	

How did you do?

Score.................. Time..................

8

Name ....

Draw lines to join up both parts of the times table. One has been done for you.

1
a	7 x 2	16
b	8 x 2	10
c	5 x 2	12
d	6 x 2	14

2
a	6 x 2	10
b	5 x 2	14
c	8 x 2	12
d	7 x 2	16

3

7 x 2   5 x 2   14   12

8 x 2   6 x 2   10   16

4

10   6 x 2   16   7 x 2

8 x 2   14   5 x 2   12

How did you do?   Score.................. Time..................

9

Name ....

Fill in the answers on Spikey's legs where there is a space.

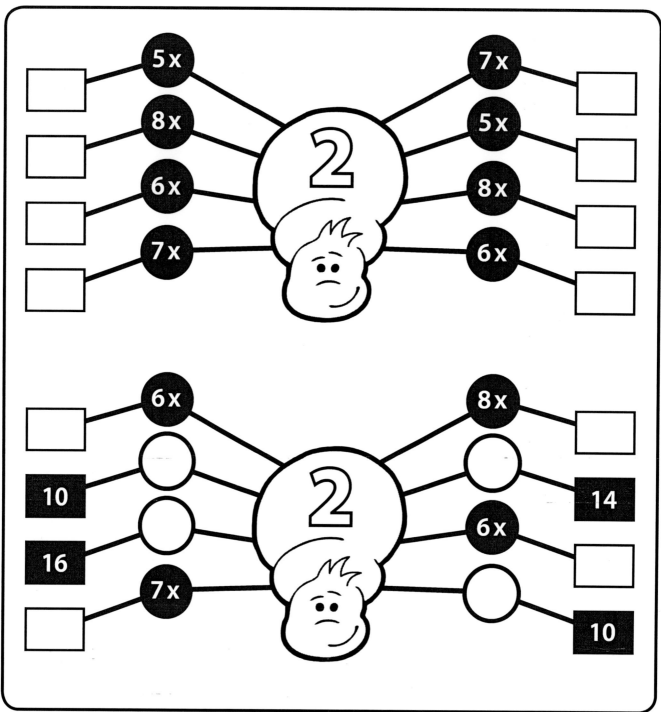

How did you do?

Score................ Time................

© Copyright HeadStart Primary Ltd

Name ....

Tabby the Table Dragon here. You are doing really well! Now let's join the two parts together.

Listen to Track 5 and try to join in! Then try to put the answers in on Track 6.

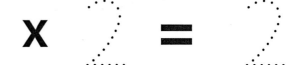

1 X 2 = 2

2 X 2 = 4

3 X 2 = 6

4 X 2 = 8

5 X 2 = 10

6 X 2 = 12

7 X 2 = 14

8 X 2 = 16

◯ minutes!

Hello again! Try to put the correct answers in the empty boxes in the time given.

1

a	1 x 2 =	☐
b	2 x 2 =	☐
c	3 x 2 =	☐
d	4 x 2 =	☐
e	5 x 2 =	☐
f	6 x 2 =	☐
g	7 x 2 =	☐
h	8 x 2 =	☐

2

a	8 x 2 =	☐
b	7 x 2 =	☐
c	6 x 2 =	☐
d	5 x 2 =	☐
e	4 x 2 =	☐
f	3 x 2 =	☐
g	2 x 2 =	☐
h	1 x 2 =	☐

3

a	4 x 2 =	☐
b	7 x 2 =	☐
c	2 x 2 =	☐
d	5 x 2 =	☐
e	8 x 2 =	☐
f	3 x 2 =	☐
g	1 x 2 =	☐
h	6 x 2 =	☐

4

a	3 x 2 =	☐
b	☐ x 2 = 12
c	1 x ☐ = 2
d	☐ x 2 = 8
e	8 x 2 = ☐
f	☐ x 2 = 10
g	2 x ☐ = 4
h	☐ x 2 = 14

How did you do?

Score.................. Time..................

12

Name ....

See if you can find all the answers in the time given.

 minutes!

1
a. 2 x 2 =
b. 5 x 2 =
c. 8 x 2 =
d. 3 x 2 =
e. 1 x 2 =
f. 6 x 2 =
g. 4 x 2 =
h. 7 x 2 =

2
a. = 8 x 2
b. = 1 x 2
c. = 4 x 2
d. = 2 x 2
e. = 5 x 2
f. = 3 x 2
g. = 7 x 2
h. = 6 x 2

3
a. x 2 = 8
b. x 2 = 2
c. x 2 = 16
d. x 2 = 12
e. x 2 = 6
f. x 2 = 10
g. x 2 = 4
h. x 2 = 14

4
a. 3 x 2 =
b. x 2 = 14
c. = 5 x 2
d. 4 = x 2
e. 1 x = 2
f. = 8 x 2
g. 4 x 2 =
h. 12 = x 2

How did you do?

Score.................. Time..................

13

Name ....

You are doing well! Now let's see if you can join the two parts with a line. One has been done for you.

1

a	1 x 2	14
b	2 x 2	8
c	3 x 2	2
d	4 x 2	10
e	5 x 2	4
f	6 x 2	16
g	7 x 2	6
h	8 x 2	12

2

a	4 x 2	2
b	7 x 2	16
c	2 x 2	12
d	5 x 2	6
e	8 x 2	4
f	3 x 2	8
g	6 x 2	14
h	1 x 2	10

3

8 x 2   6   2   6 x 2

4   4 x 2   14   5 x 2   8

1 x 2   12   16   7 x 2

2 x 2   10   3 x 2

How did you do?

Score.................. Time..................

© Copyright HeadStart Primary Ltd

14

Spikey's here again! See if you can write the answers on his legs.

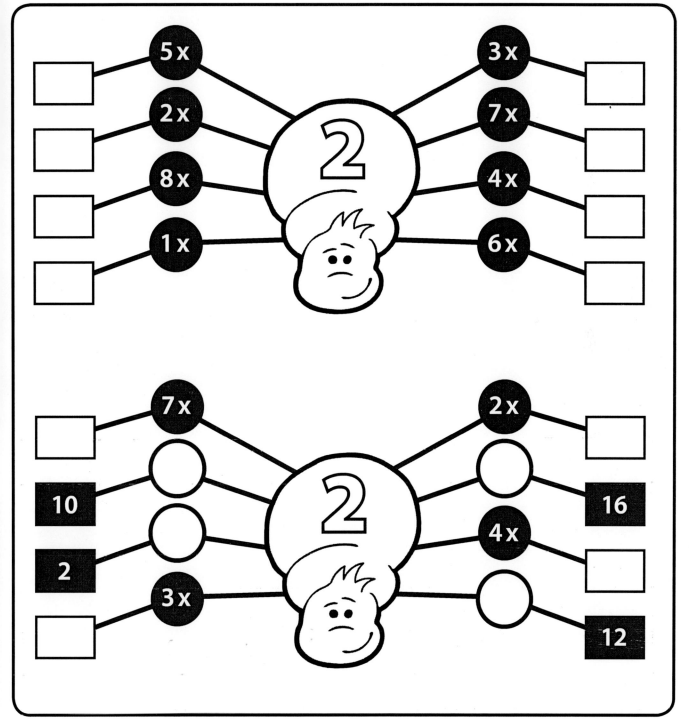

How did you do?   Score.................. Time..................

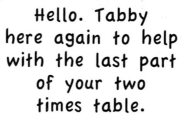

Hello. Tabby here again to help with the last part of your two times table.

Listen to Tracks 7 and 8 and join in when you are ready.

9 X 2 = 18

10 X 2 = 20

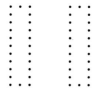   

11 X 2 = 22

12 X 2 = 24

Name ....

Hi. Can you fill in the spaces with the correct numbers?

1
a) 9 x 2 = ☐
b) 10 x 2 = ☐
c) 11 x 2 = ☐
d) 12 x 2 = ☐

2
a) 9 x 2 = ☐
b) 10 x 2 = ☐
c) 11 x 2 = ☐
d) 12 x 2 = ☐

3
a) ☐ x 2 = 18
b) ☐ x 2 = 20
c) ☐ x 2 = 22
d) ☐ x 2 = 24

4
a) ☐ x 2 = 18
b) 10 x ☐ = 20
c) ☐ x 2 = 22
d) 12 x 2 = ☐

How did you do?

Score.................. Time..................

17

Name ....

◯ minutes!

Now you need to test yourself. See how many you can get right in the time given.

1
a) 9 x 2 =
b) 10 x 2 =
c) 11 x 2 =
d) 12 x 2 =
e) 11 x 2 =
f) 10 x 2 =
g) 9 x 2 =
h) 12 x 2 =

2
a) 11 x 2 =
b) 12 x 2 =
c) 10 x 2 =
d) 9 x 2 =
e) 12 x 2 =
f) 10 x 2 =
g) 11 x 2 =
h) 9 x 2 =

3
a) 10 x 2 =
b) 12 x 2 =
c) 11 x 2 =
d) 10 x 2 =
e) 9 x 2 =
f) 11 x 2 =
g) 9 x 2 =
h) 12 x 2 =

4
a) 9 x 2 =
b) 11 x 2 =
c) 10 x 2 =
d) 9 x 2 =
e) 12 x 2 =
f) 10 x 2 =
g) 11 x 2 =
h) 9 x 2 =

How did you do?

Score.................. Time..................

© Copyright HeadStart Primary Ltd

18

Name ....

Draw lines now to join up both parts of the times table. One has been done for you.

1
a 10 x 2 → 22
b 12 x 2 — 18
c 9 x 2 → 20
d 11 x 2 — 24

2
a 11 x 2 — 24
b 10 x 2 — 18
c 12 x 2 — 22
d 9 x 2 — 20

3
| 22 | 24 |

| 20 | 18 |

9 x 2   11 x 2

10 x 2   12 x 2

4
11 x 2   18   10 x 2   22

20   9 x 2   24   12 x 2

How did you do?   ☹   Score................. Time.................

© Copyright HeadStart Primary Ltd   **19**

Name ....

How did you do?

Score.................. Time..................

20

Hello. It's Tabby the Table Dragon here. You are doing really well!

Let's put all the parts together and try to chant the whole two times table. Listen to Tracks 9 and 10 and join in when you are ready.

Draw over all the numbers with a coloured pencil or felt tip

1 X 2 = 2

2 X 2 = 4

3 X 2 = 6

4 X 2 = 8

5 X 2 = 10

6 X 2 = 12

7 X 2 = 14

8 X 2 = 16

9 X 2 = 18

10 X 2 = 20

11 X 2 = 22

12 X 2 = 24

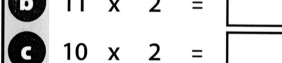

Hello. Try to put
the correct answers
in the empty boxes.
Sets 3 and 4 are on
the next page.

1

a	1	x	2	=	☐
b	2	x	2	=	☐
c	3	x	2	=	☐
d	4	x	2	=	☐
e	5	x	2	=	☐
f	6	x	2	=	☐
g	7	x	2	=	☐
h	8	x	2	=	☐
i	9	x	2	=	☐
j	10	x	2	=	☐
k	11	x	2	=	☐
l	12	x	2	=	☐

2

a	12	x	2	=	☐
b	11	x	2	=	☐
c	10	x	2	=	☐
d	9	x	2	=	☐
e	8	x	2	=	☐
f	7	x	2	=	☐
g	6	x	2	=	☐
h	5	x	2	=	☐
i	4	x	2	=	☐
j	3	x	2	=	☐
k	2	x	2	=	☐
l	1	x	2	=	☐

How did you do?

Score................. Time.................

Name ....

3

a 7 x 2 =
b 1 x 2 =
c 3 x 2 =
d 12 x 2 =
e 9 x 2 =
f 6 x 2 =
g 11 x 2 =
h 2 x 2 =
i 8 x 2 =
j 4 x 2 =
k 10 x 2 =
l 5 x 2 =

4

a 3 x 2 =
b ☐ x 2 = 10
c ☐ x 2 = 22
d 8 x 2 =
e ☐ x 2 = 24
f 7 x 2 =
g 10 x 2 =
h ☐ x 2 = 4
i ☐ x 2 = 18
j 1 x 2 =
k ☐ x 2 = 8
l 6 x 2 =

Well done; you're doing a great job!

How did you do?

Score.................. Time..................

© Copyright HeadStart Primary Ltd   23

It's race time! Try to beat the clock. See if you can find all the answers in the time given. Try to complete all 4 sets.

minutes!

1

a. 11 x 2 = ☐

b. 2 x 2 = ☐

c. 5 x 2 = ☐

d. 10 x 2 = ☐

e. 3 x 2 = ☐

f. 8 x 2 = ☐

g. 6 x 2 = ☐

h. 1 x 2 = ☐

i. 12 x 2 = ☐

j. 7 x 2 = ☐

k. 4 x 2 = ☐

l. 9 x 2 = ☐

2

a. ☐ x 2 = 16

b. ☐ x 2 = 2

c. ☐ x 2 = 8

d. ☐ x 2 = 24

e. ☐ x 2 = 4

f. ☐ x 2 = 10

g. ☐ x 2 = 22

h. ☐ x 2 = 6

i. ☐ x 2 = 14

j. ☐ x 2 = 18

k. ☐ x 2 = 12

l. ☐ x 2 = 20

Turn to the next page

3

a   ☐ = 3 x 2

b   ☐ = 7 x 2

c   ☐ = 10 x 2

d   ☐ = 5 x 2

e   ☐ = 2 x 2

f   ☐ = 12 x 2

g   ☐ = 8 x 2

h   ☐ = 1 x 2

i   ☐ = 11 x 2

j   ☐ = 6 x 2

k   ☐ = 9 x 2

l   ☐ = 4 x 2

4

a   4 x 2 = ☐

b   ☐ x 2 = 20

c   1 x ☐ = 2

d   ☐ x 2 = 12

e   ☐ = 12 x 2

f   3 x ☐ = 6

g   8 x 2 = ☐

h   10 = ☐ x 2

i   ☐ x 2 = 22

j   2 x ☐ = 4

k   ☐ = 9 x 2

l   ☐ x 2 = 14

Take care...
some of them
have been
turned around.

How did you do?

Score.................. Time..................

Name ....

You are doing really well! Let's see if you can join the two parts with a line. One has been done for you.

1

a	1 x 2	12
b	2 x 2	18
c	3 x 2	10
d	4 x 2	2
e	5 x 2	6
f	6 x 2	24
g	7 x 2	4
h	8 x 2	22
i	9 x 2	20
j	10 x 2	8
k	11 x 2	16
l	12 x 2	14

2

a	7 x 2	2
b	5 x 2	20
c	1 x 2	6
d	12 x 2	14
e	4 x 2	18
f	3 x 2	10
g	10 x 2	4
h	6 x 2	24
i	9 x 2	8
j	2 x 2	16
k	11 x 2	12
l	8 x 2	22

How did you do?

Score.................. Time..................

26

Name ....

See if you can join each dragon egg to the correct diamond. One has been done for you.

3

10 x 2   6   22   6 x 2

3 x 2   16   9 x 2   8 x 2

24   5 x 2   20   4

4 x 2   8   2 x 2   18

12 x 2   12   11 x 2   7 x 2

10   1 x 2   14   2

How did you do?   Score................. Time.................

© Copyright HeadStart Primary Ltd   27

Name ....

FIND MY CAVE

HOME SWEET HOME

FINISH

START

Join the answers to the two times table, in the correct order, to find the path to my cave.

© Copyright HeadStart Primary Ltd

28

Name ....

COLOUR A DINOSAUR

Can you use your two times table to colour in my dinosaur friends correctly?

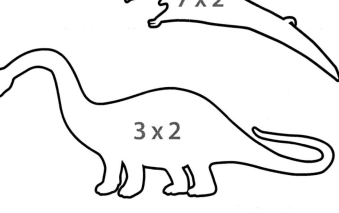

7 x 2

9 x 2

3 x 2

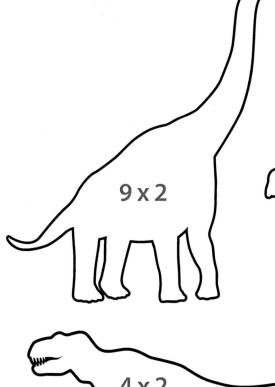

4 x 2

12 x 2

8 x 2

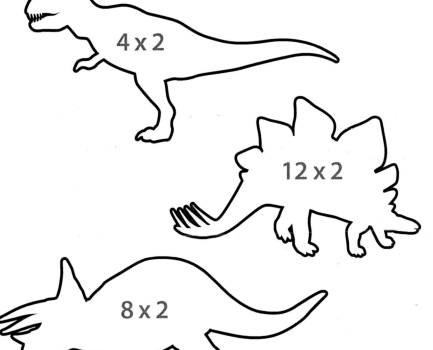

16	– Red
24	– Yellow
8	– Purple
14	– Brown
6	– Green
18	– Blue

Game time! You need the next page and a partner to play this game.

PICK UP A PAIR

1 Cut along the lines around the numbers. Separate the cards into questions and answers.

2 Turn the cut out shapes over on a table so that you cannot see the numbers and then mix them up. Keep the groups separate.

3 Take it in turns to turn over two shapes, one from the questions and one from the answers.

4 If the question and answer match, keep the cards, and have another go.

5 If the question and answer does not match, turn the cards back over. Your partner then has a go.

6 The player with the most pairs at the end is the winner.

1×2	2×2	3×2
4×2	5×2	6×2
7×2	8×2	9×2
10×2	11×2	12×2
2	4	6
8	10	12
14	16	18
20	22	24

The

5

times table

CONTENTS: 5 times tables

BOOK CONTENTS

CD CONTENTS

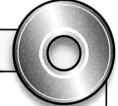

Hello! I'm Tabby the Table Dragon. I am going to help you learn your five times table.

Listen to Track 14 on the CD. Take note of the rhythm and join in when you are ready. Then try to put in the answers on Track 15.

$$1 \times 5 = 5$$

$$2 \times 5 = 10$$

$$3 \times 5 = 15$$

$$4 \times 5 = 20$$

Hello! Tabby the Table Dragon here! Can you fill in the spaces with the correct numbers?

1
a	1 x 5 =	☐
b	2 x 5 =	☐
c	3 x 5 =	☐
d	4 x 5 =	☐

2
a	1 x 5 =	☐
b	2 x 5 =	☐
c	3 x 5 =	☐
d	4 x 5 =	☐

3
a	☐ x 5 = 5
b	☐ x 5 = 10
c	☐ x 5 = 15
d	☐ x 5 = 20

4
a	☐ x 5 = 5
b	2 x ☐ = 10
c	☐ x 5 = 15
d	4 x 5 = ☐

How did you do?

Score................. Time.................

Name ....

Now you are going to get a score. See how many you can get right in the time given.

◯ minutes!

1
a. 2 x 5 = ☐
b. 4 x 5 = ☐
c. 1 x 5 = ☐
d. 3 x 5 = ☐
e. 4 x 5 = ☐
f. 2 x 5 = ☐
g. 3 x 5 = ☐
h. 1 x 5 = ☐

2
a. 4 x 5 = ☐
b. 1 x 5 = ☐
c. 3 x 5 = ☐
d. 2 x 5 = ☐
e. 1 x 5 = ☐
f. 3 x 5 = ☐
g. 2 x 5 = ☐
h. 4 x 5 = ☐

3
a. 1 x 5 = ☐
b. 4 x 5 = ☐
c. 2 x 5 = ☐
d. 3 x 5 = ☐
e. 4 x 5 = ☐
f. 1 x 5 = ☐
g. 3 x 5 = ☐
h. 2 x 5 = ☐

4
a. 3 x 5 = ☐
b. 1 x 5 = ☐
c. 4 x 5 = ☐
d. 2 x 5 = ☐
e. 1 x 5 = ☐
f. 4 x 5 = ☐
g. 3 x 5 = ☐
h. 2 x 5 = ☐

How did you do?

Score................. Time.................

Name ....

On this page draw lines to join up the two parts of the times table. One has been done for you.

1
a	4 x 5	→	15
b	1 x 5		10
c	3 x 5	→	20
d	2 x 5		5

2
a	3 x 5		5
b	4 x 5		15
c	2 x 5		20
d	1 x 5		10

3

2 x 5   1 x 5   15   20

4 x 5   3 x 5   10   5

4

10   4 x 5   5   3 x 5

1 x 5   15   2 x 5   20

How did you do?   Score.................. Time..................

4

See if you can work out the answers on Olly the Octopus's tentacles.

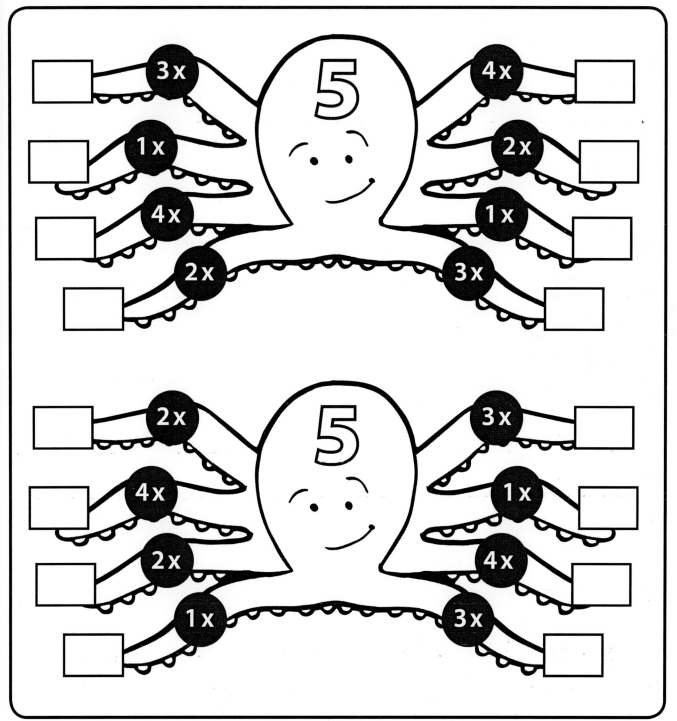

How did you do?   Score.................... Time....................

Tabby here.
Well done! Let's
move on to the
next part.

Listen to Track 16
on the CD and join in
when you are ready.
Then try and put
the answers in on
Track 17.

5 x 5 = 25

6 x 5 = 30

7 x 5 = 35

8 x 5 = 40

Hi. Try to fill in the spaces with the correct numbers.

1
- **a** 5 x 5 = ☐
- **b** 6 x 5 = ☐
- **c** 7 x 5 = ☐
- **d** 8 x 5 = ☐

2
- **a** 5 x 5 = ☐
- **b** 6 x 5 = ☐
- **c** 7 x 5 = ☐
- **d** 8 x 5 = ☐

3
- **a** ☐ x 5 = 25
- **b** ☐ x 5 = 30
- **c** ☐ x 5 = 35
- **d** ☐ x 5 = 40

4
- **a** ☐ x 5 = 25
- **b** 6 x ☐ = 30
- **c** ☐ x 5 = 35
- **d** 8 x 5 = ☐

How did you do?

Score.................. Time..................

Name ....

○ **minutes!**

This time, see if you can get them all right in the time given.

1
a 6 x 5 = ☐
b 8 x 5 = ☐
c 5 x 5 = ☐
d 7 x 5 = ☐
e 8 x 5 = ☐
f 6 x 5 = ☐
g 7 x 5 = ☐
h 5 x 5 = ☐

2
a 7 x 5 = ☐
b 5 x 5 = ☐
c 8 x 5 = ☐
d 6 x 5 = ☐
e 5 x 5 = ☐
f 8 x 5 = ☐
g 7 x 5 = ☐
h 6 x 5 = ☐

3
a 5 x 5 = ☐
b 8 x 5 = ☐
c 6 x 5 = ☐
d 7 x 5 = ☐
e 8 x 5 = ☐
f 5 x 5 = ☐
g 7 x 5 = ☐
h 6 x 5 = ☐

4
a 8 x 5 = ☐
b 5 x 5 = ☐
c 7 x 5 = ☐
d 6 x 5 = ☐
e 5 x 5 = ☐
f 7 x 5 = ☐
g 6 x 5 = ☐
h 8 x 5 = ☐

How did you do?

Score.................. Time..................

8

Name ....

Draw lines to join up both parts of the times table. One has been done for you.

1
a	6 x 5	25
b	5 x 5	35
c	8 x 5	30
d	7 x 5	40

2
a	7 x 5	40
b	8 x 5	25
c	5 x 5	30
d	6 x 5	35

3

8 x 5   6 x 5   25   40

7 x 5   5 x 5   35   30

4

25   6 x 5   40   7 x 5

8 x 5   35   5 x 5   30

How did you do?   Score.................. Time..................

See if you can work out the answers on Olly the Octopus's tentacles.

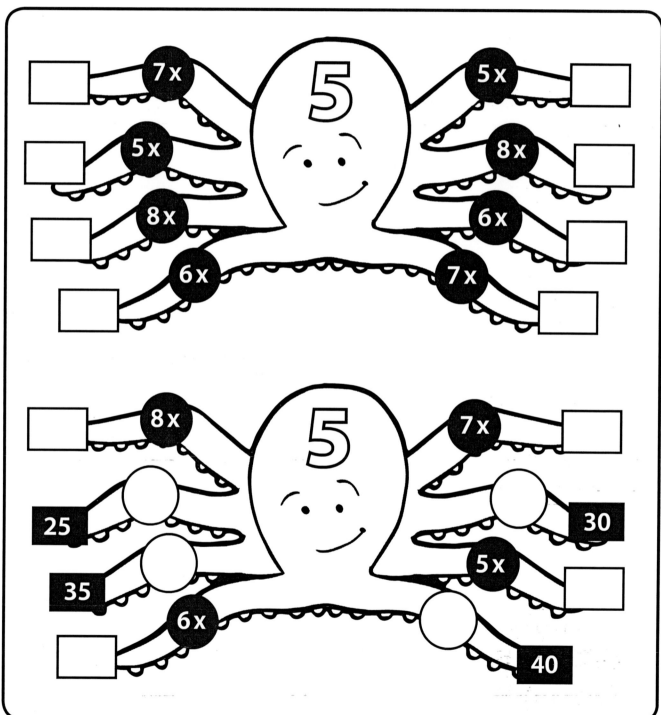

How did you do?

10

Name ....

Tabby the Table Dragon here. You are doing really well! Now let's join the two parts together.

Listen to Track 18 and try to join in! Then try to put the answers in on Track 19.

1 x 5 = 5

2 x 5 = 10

3 x 5 = 15

4 x 5 = 20

5 x 5 = 25

6 x 5 = 30

7 x 5 = 35

8 x 5 = 40

Join up the dots to write the numbers

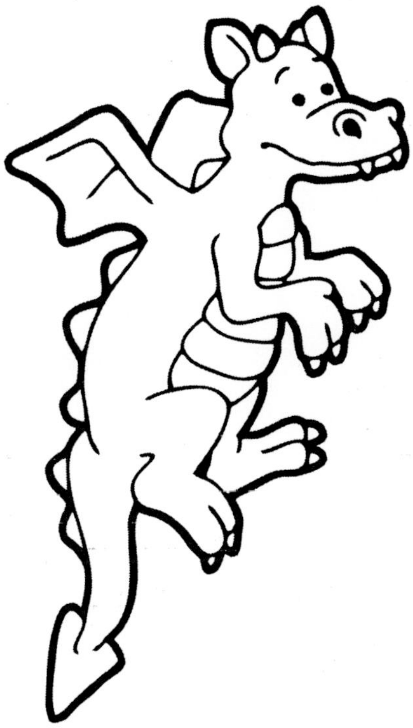

◯ minutes!

Hello again! Try to put the correct answers in the empty boxes in the time given.

1
- **a** 1 x 5 = ▢
- **b** 2 x 5 = ▢
- **c** 3 x 5 = ▢
- **d** 4 x 5 = ▢
- **e** 5 x 5 = ▢
- **f** 6 x 5 = ▢
- **g** 7 x 5 = ▢
- **h** 8 x 5 = ▢

2
- **a** 8 x 5 = ▢
- **b** 7 x 5 = ▢
- **c** 6 x 5 = ▢
- **d** 5 x 5 = ▢
- **e** 4 x 5 = ▢
- **f** 3 x 5 = ▢
- **g** 2 x 5 = ▢
- **h** 1 x 5 = ▢

3
- **a** 2 x 5 = ▢
- **b** 5 x 5 = ▢
- **c** 8 x 5 = ▢
- **d** 3 x 5 = ▢
- **e** 1 x 5 = ▢
- **f** 6 x 5 = ▢
- **g** 4 x 5 = ▢
- **h** 7 x 5 = ▢

4
- **a** 6 x 5 = ▢
- **b** ▢ x 5 = 15
- **c** 1 x ▢ = 5
- **d** ▢ x 5 = 20
- **e** 8 x 5 = ▢
- **f** ▢ x 5 = 25
- **g** 2 x ▢ = 10
- **h** ▢ x 5 = 35

How did you do?

Score.................. Time..................

See if you can find all the answers in the time given.

Name ....

 minutes!

1
a) 3 x 5 = ☐
b) 1 x 5 = ☐
c) 6 x 5 = ☐
d) 4 x 5 = ☐
e) 7 x 5 = ☐
f) 2 x 5 = ☐
g) 8 x 5 = ☐
h) 5 x 5 = ☐

2
a) ☐ = 4 x 5
b) ☐ = 2 x 5
c) ☐ = 5 x 5
d) ☐ = 3 x 5
e) ☐ = 7 x 5
f) ☐ = 6 x 5
g) ☐ = 8 x 5
h) ☐ = 1 x 5

3
a) ☐ x 5 = 15
b) ☐ x 5 = 25
c) ☐ x 5 = 10
d) ☐ x 5 = 35
e) ☐ x 5 = 20
f) ☐ x 5 = 5
g) ☐ x 5 = 40
h) ☐ x 5 = 30

4
a) 7 x 5 = ☐
b) ☐ x 5 = 10
c) ☐ = 5 x 5
d) 15 = ☐ x 5
e) 1 x 5 = ☐
f) ☐ = 8 x 5
g) 4 x 5 = ☐
h) 30 = ☐ x 5

How did you do?

Score.................. Time..................

13

Name ....

You are doing well! Now let's see if you can join the two parts with a line. One has been done for you.

1

a	1 x 5	35
b	2 x 5	20
c	3 x 5	5
d	4 x 5	25
e	5 x 5	10
f	6 x 5	40
g	7 x 5	15
h	8 x 5	30

2

a	7 x 5	40
b	2 x 5	30
c	5 x 5	15
d	8 x 5	10
e	3 x 5	20
f	6 x 5	35
g	1 x 5	25
h	4 x 5	5

3

7 x 5   15   40   1 x 5

10   4 x 5   5   5 x 5   20

6 x 5   25   35   8 x 5

2 x 5   30   3 x 5

How did you do?   Score.................. Time..................

© Copyright HeadStart Primary Ltd

14

Name ....

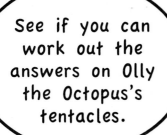
See if you can work out the answers on Olly the Octopus's tentacles.

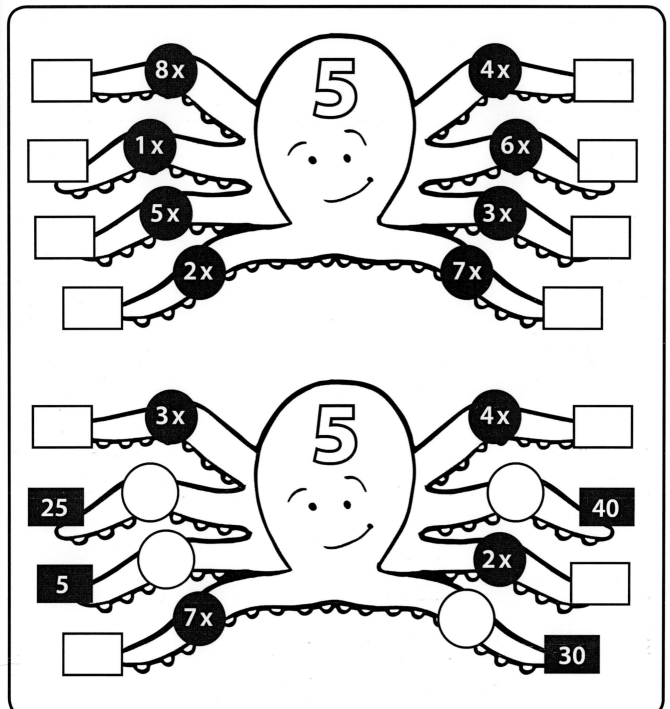

How did you do?   Score.................. Time..................

© Copyright HeadStart Primary Ltd   15

Hello. Tabby here again to help with the last part of your five times table.

Listen to Tracks 20 and 21 and join in when you are ready.

$$9 \times 5 = 45$$

$$10 \times 5 = 50$$

$$11 \times 5 = 55$$

$$12 \times 5 = 60$$

Hi. Can you fill in the spaces with the correct numbers?

1
a) 9 x 5 = ☐
b) 10 x 5 = ☐
c) 11 x 5 = ☐
d) 12 x 5 = ☐

2
a) 9 x 5 = ☐
b) 10 x 5 = ☐
c) 11 x 5 = ☐
d) 12 x 5 = ☐

3
a) ☐ x 5 = 45
b) ☐ x 5 = 50
c) ☐ x 5 = 55
d) ☐ x 5 = 60

4
a) ☐ x 5 = 45
b) 10 x ☐ = 50
c) ☐ x 5 = 55
d) 12 x 5 = ☐

How did you do?

Score................. Time.................

Name ....

○ minutes!

Now you need to test yourself. See how many you can get right in the time given.

1
a   9   x   5   =   ☐
b   10   x   5   =   ☐
c   11   x   5   =   ☐
d   12   x   5   =   ☐
e   9   x   5   =   ☐
f   10   x   5   =   ☐
g   11   x   5   =   ☐
h   12   x   5   =   ☐

2
a   12   x   5   =   ☐
b   11   x   5   =   ☐
c   10   x   5   =   ☐
d   9   x   5   =   ☐
e   12   x   5   =   ☐
f   11   x   5   =   ☐
g   10   x   5   =   ☐
h   9   x   5   =   ☐

3
a   10   x   5   =   ☐
b   12   x   5   =   ☐
c   11   x   5   =   ☐
d   9   x   5   =   ☐
e   11   x   5   =   ☐
f   10   x   5   =   ☐
g   9   x   5   =   ☐
h   12   x   5   =   ☐

4
a   9   x   5   =   ☐
b   12   x   5   =   ☐
c   10   x   5   =   ☐
d   11   x   5   =   ☐
e   12   x   5   =   ☐
f   10   x   5   =   ☐
g   11   x   5   =   ☐
h   9   x   5   =   ☐

How did you do?

Score................. Time.................

18

Name ....

Draw lines now to join up both parts of the times table. One has been done for you.

1
a	9 x 5	50
b	11 x 5	60
c	10 x 5	55
d	12 x 5	45

2
a	12 x 5	55
b	9 x 5	50
c	11 x 5	60
d	10 x 5	45

3

50   45

55   60

10 x 5   12 x 5

9 x 5   11 x 5

4

12 x 5   45   10 x 5   60

50   9 x 5   55   11 x 5

How did you do?   Score.................. Time..................

19

See if you can work out the answers on Olly the Octopus's tentacles.

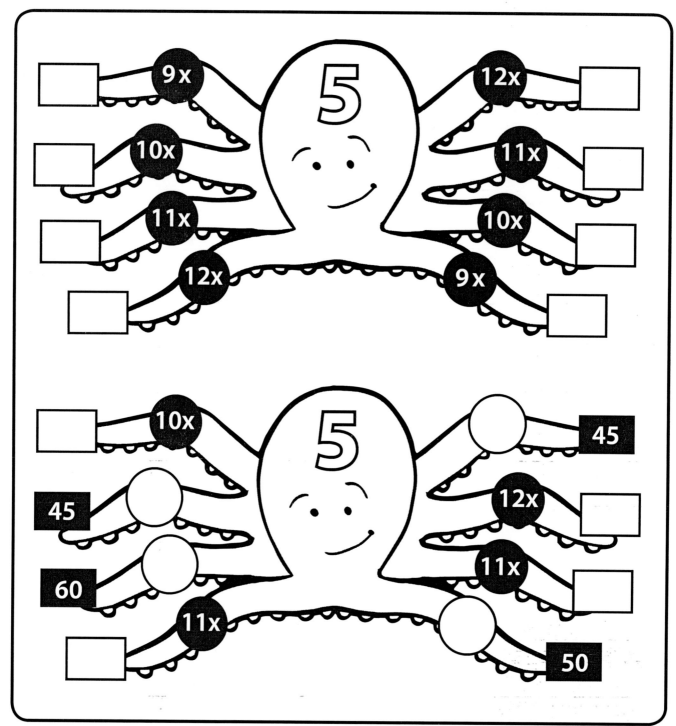

How did you do?   Score.................. Time..................

Hello. It's Tabby the Table Dragon here. You are doing really well!

Let's put all the parts together and try to chant the whole five times table. Listen to Tracks 22 and 23 and join in when you are ready.

Draw over all the numbers with a coloured pencil or felt tip

1 X 5 = 5

2 X 5 = 10

3 X 5 = 15

4 X 5 = 20

5 X 5 = 25

6 X 5 = 30

7 X 5 = 35

8 X 5 = 40

9 X 5 = 45

10 X 5 = 50

11 X 5 = 55

12 X 5 = 60

21

Name ....

Hello. Try to put the correct answers in the empty boxes. Sets 3 and 4 are on the next page.

1

a   1   x   5   =   ☐

b   2   x   5   =   ☐

c   3   x   5   =   ☐

d   4   x   5   =   ☐

e   5   x   5   =   ☐

f   6   x   5   =   ☐

g   7   x   5   =   ☐

h   8   x   5   =   ☐

i   9   x   5   =   ☐

j   10   x   5   =   ☐

k   11   x   5   =   ☐

l   12   x   5   =   ☐

2

a   12   x   5   =   ☐

b   11   x   5   =   ☐

c   10   x   5   =   ☐

d   9   x   5   =   ☐

e   8   x   5   =   ☐

f   7   x   5   =   ☐

g   6   x   5   =   ☐

h   5   x   5   =   ☐

i   4   x   5   =   ☐

j   3   x   5   =   ☐

k   2   x   5   =   ☐

l   1   x   5   =   ☐

How did you do?

Score.................. Time..................

Name ....

3

a	6	x 5	=	☐
b	11	x 5	=	☐
c	2	x 5	=	☐
d	8	x 5	=	☐
e	4	x 5	=	☐
f	10	x 5	=	☐
g	5	x 5	=	☐
h	7	x 5	=	☐
i	1	x 5	=	☐
j	3	x 5	=	☐
k	12	x 5	=	☐
l	9	x 5	=	☐

4

a	7	x 5	=	☐
b	10	x 5	=	☐
c	☐	x 5	=	10
d	☐	x 5	=	45
e	1	x 5	=	☐
f	☐	x 5	=	20
g	6	x 5	=	☐
h	3	x 5	=	☐
i	☐	x 5	=	25
j	☐	x 5	=	55
k	8	x 5	=	☐
l	☐	x 5	=	60

Well done; you're doing a great job!

How did you do?

Score.................. Time..................

© Copyright HeadStart Primary Ltd

23

It's race time!
Try to beat the clock. See if you can find all the answers in the time given. Try to complete all 4 sets.

minutes!

1

a	6	x	5	=	
b	1	x	5	=	
c	12	x	5	=	
d	7	x	5	=	
e	4	x	5	=	
f	9	x	5	=	
g	11	x	5	=	
h	2	x	5	=	
i	5	x	5	=	
j	10	x	5	=	
k	3	x	5	=	
l	8	x	5	=	

2

a		x	5	=	25
b		x	5	=	60
c		x	5	=	15
d		x	5	=	50
e		x	5	=	45
f		x	5	=	30
g		x	5	=	55
h		x	5	=	40
i		x	5	=	5
j		x	5	=	20
k		x	5	=	35
l		x	5	=	10

Turn to the next page

3

a □ = 10 x 5
b □ = 5 x 5
c □ = 2 x 5
d □ = 12 x 5
e □ = 8 x 5
f □ = 1 x 5
g □ = 11 x 5
h □ = 6 x 5
i □ = 9 x 5
j □ = 4 x 5
k □ = 3 x 5
l □ = 7 x 5

4

a 12 x 5 = □
b 3 x □ = 15
c 8 x 5 = □
d 25 = □ x 5
e □ x 5 = 55
f 2 x □ = 10
g 9 x 5 = □
h 35 = □ x 5
i 4 x 5 = □
j □ x 5 = 50
k 1 x □ = 5
l 30 = □ x 5

Take care...
some of them
have been
turned around.

How did you do?

Score................. Time.................

Name ....

You are doing really well! Let's see if you can join the two parts with a line. One has been done for you.

1

a	1 x 5	30
b	2 x 5	45
c	3 x 5	25
d	4 x 5	5
e	5 x 5	60
f	6 x 5	15
g	7 x 5	40
h	8 x 5	55
i	9 x 5	20
j	10 x 5	50
k	11 x 5	35
l	12 x 5	10

2

a	4 x 5	45
b	3 x 5	25
c	10 x 5	10
d	6 x 5	60
e	9 x 5	20
f	2 x 5	55
g	11 x 5	40
h	8 x 5	5
i	7 x 5	30
j	5 x 5	15
k	12 x 5	50
l	1 x 5	35

How did you do?

Score.................. Time..................

26

Name ....

See if you can join each dragon egg to the correct diamond. One has been done for you.

3

2 x 5

15

40

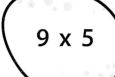
9 x 5

30

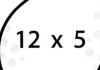
12 x 5

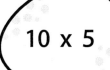
10 x 5

3 x 5

50

5 x 5

55

45

4 x 5

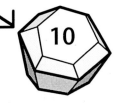
10

8 x 5

25

20

6 x 5

7 x 5

11 x 5

1 x 5

35

60

5

How did you do?   Score.................. Time..................

CRACK THE CODE

Use your code-cracking skills to work out the secret message!

F	S	R	I	V	L	A
5	10	15	20	25	30	35

M	E	B	T	!
40	45	50	55	60

4 x 5

7 x 5	8 x 5

7 x 5

1 x 5	4 x 5	5 x 5	9 x 5

11 x 5	4 x 5	8 x 5	9 x 5	2 x 5

11 x 5	7 x 5	10 x 5	6 x 5	9 x 5

2 x 5	11 x 5	7 x 5	3 x 5	12 x 5

The

10

times table

CONTENTS: 10 times tables

BOOK CONTENTS

CD CONTENTS

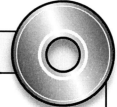

Hello! I'm Tabby the Table Dragon. I am going to help you learn your ten times table.

Listen to Track 27 on the CD. Take note of the rhythm and join in when you are ready. Then try to put in the answers on Track 28.

1 x 10 = 10

2 x 10 = 20

3 x 10 = 30

4 x 10 = 40

1

Hello! Tabby the Table Dragon here! Can you fill in the spaces with the correct numbers?

1
a) 1 x 10 = ☐
b) 2 x 10 = ☐
c) 3 x 10 = ☐
d) 4 x 10 = ☐

2
a) 1 x 10 = ☐
b) 2 x 10 = ☐
c) 3 x 10 = ☐
d) 4 x 10 = ☐

3
a) ☐ x 10 = 10
b) ☐ x 10 = 20
c) ☐ x 10 = 30
d) ☐ x 10 = 40

4
a) ☐ x 10 = 10
b) 2 x ☐ = 20
c) ☐ x 10 = 30
d) 4 x 10 = ☐

How did you do?

Score.................. Time..................

Name ....

Now you are going to get a score. See how many you can get right in the time given.

 minutes!

1
a   4 x 10 =
b   1 x 10 =
c   3 x 10 =
d   2 x 10 =
e   1 x 10 =
f   4 x 10 =
g   2 x 10 =
h   3 x 10 =

2
a   3 x 10 =
b   1 x 10 =
c   4 x 10 =
d   2 x 10 =
e   1 x 10 =
f   3 x 10 =
g   2 x 10 =
h   4 x 10 =

3
a   1 x 10 =
b   3 x 10 =
c   2 x 10 =
d   4 x 10 =
e   3 x 10 =
f   2 x 10 =
g   4 x 10 =
h   1 x 10 =

4
a   2 x 10 =
b   4 x 10 =
c   1 x 10 =
d   3 x 10 =
e   4 x 10 =
f   2 x 10 =
g   3 x 10 =
h   1 x 10 =

How did you do?

Score.................. Time..................

3

Name ....

On this page draw lines to join up the two parts of the times table. One has been done to help you.

1
a 2 x 10 → 10
b 1 x 10 30
c 4 x 10 20
d 3 x 10 40

2
a 3 x 10 20
b 4 x 10 10
c 1 x 10 40
d 2 x 10 30

3
1 x 10   3 x 10   20   40
4 x 10   2 x 10   30   10

4
40   1 x 10   30   2 x 10
3 x 10   20   4 x 10   10

How did you do?

Score................. Time.................

4

Name ....

See if you can work out the answers on Spikey the Spider's legs.

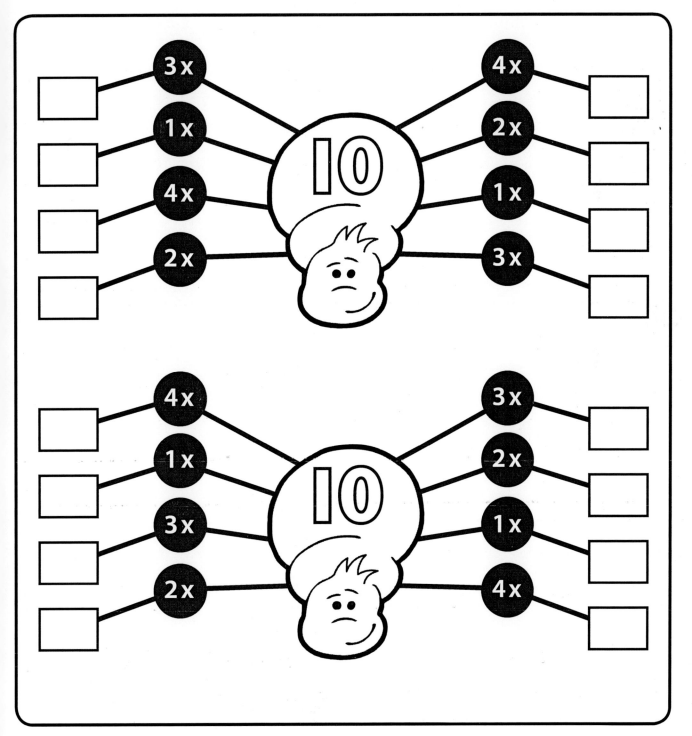

How did you do?   Score................. Time.................

© Copyright HeadStart Primary Ltd

5

Tabby here. Well done! Let's move on to the next part.

Listen to Track 29 on the CD and join in when you are ready. Then try and put the answers in on Track 30.

$$5 \times 10 = 50$$

$$6 \times 10 = 60$$

$$7 \times 10 = 70$$

$$8 \times 10 = 80$$

Name ....

Hi. Try to fill in the spaces with the correct numbers.

1
a 5 x 10 = ☐
b 6 x 10 = ☐
c 7 x 10 = ☐
d 8 x 10 = ☐

2
a 5 x 10 = ☐
b 6 x 10 = ☐
c 7 x 10 = ☐
d 8 x 10 = ☐

3
a ☐ x 10 = 50
b ☐ x 10 = 60
c ☐ x 10 = 70
d ☐ x 10 = 80

4
a ☐ x 10 = 50
b 6 x ☐ = 60
c ☐ x 10 = 70
d 8 x 10 = ☐

How did you do?   Score.................. Time..................

◯ **minutes!**

> This time, see if you can get them all right in the time given.

1
a	5	x	10	= ☐
b	8	x	10	= ☐
c	6	x	10	= ☐
d	7	x	10	= ☐
e	8	x	10	= ☐
f	5	x	10	= ☐
g	7	x	10	= ☐
h	6	x	10	= ☐

2
a	7	x	10	= ☐
b	5	x	10	= ☐
c	8	x	10	= ☐
d	6	x	10	= ☐
e	5	x	10	= ☐
f	8	x	10	= ☐
g	7	x	10	= ☐
h	6	x	10	= ☐

3
a	8	x	10	= ☐
b	6	x	10	= ☐
c	7	x	10	= ☐
d	5	x	10	= ☐
e	6	x	10	= ☐
f	8	x	10	= ☐
g	5	x	10	= ☐
h	7	x	10	= ☐

4
a	6	x	10	= ☐
b	8	x	10	= ☐
c	5	x	10	= ☐
d	6	x	10	= ☐
e	8	x	10	= ☐
f	7	x	10	= ☐
g	5	x	10	= ☐
h	7	x	10	= ☐

How did you do?

Score.................. Time..................

Draw lines to join up both parts of the times table. One has been done for you.

1
a 7 x 10 → 60
b 8 x 10 → 70
c 5 x 10 → 80
d 6 x 10 → 50

2
a 5 x 10 → 70
b 8 x 10 → 50
c 7 x 10 → 60
d 6 x 10 → 80

3

8 x 10   5 x 10   60   50

7 x 10   6 x 10   70   80

4

70   8 x 10   50   6 x 10

5 x 10   60   7 x 10   80

How did you do?   Score................. Time.................

Fill in the answers on Spikey's legs where there is a space.

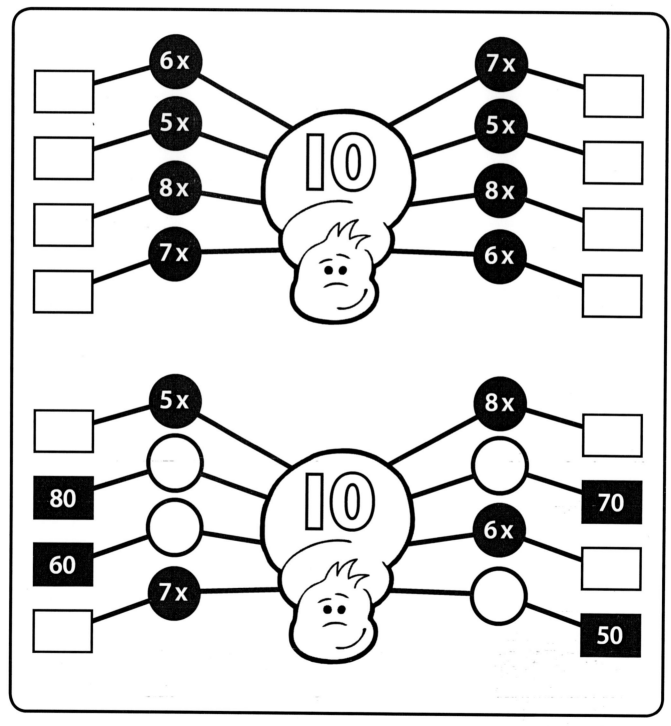

Name ....

Tabby the Table Dragon here. You are doing really well! Now let's join the two parts together.

Listen to Track 31 and try to join in! Then try to put the answers in on Track 32.

Join up the dots to write the numbers

1 X 10 = 10

2 X 10 = 20

3 X 10 = 30

4 X 10 = 40

5 X 10 = 50

6 X 10 = 60

7 X 10 = 70

8 X 10 = 80

Name ....

◯ minutes!

Hello again! Try to put the correct answers in the empty boxes in the time given.

1
a	1 x 10 =	☐
b	2 x 10 =	☐
c	3 x 10 =	☐
d	4 x 10 =	☐
e	5 x 10 =	☐
f	6 x 10 =	☐
g	7 x 10 =	☐
h	8 x 10 =	☐

2
a	8 x 10 =	☐
b	7 x 10 =	☐
c	6 x 10 =	☐
d	5 x 10 =	☐
e	4 x 10 =	☐
f	3 x 10 =	☐
g	2 x 10 =	☐
h	1 x 10 =	☐

3
a	2 x 10 =	☐
b	5 x 10 =	☐
c	8 x 10 =	☐
d	3 x 10 =	☐
e	1 x 10 =	☐
f	6 x 10 =	☐
g	4 x 10 =	☐
h	7 x 10 =	☐

4
a	☐ x 10 =	40
b	8 x 10 =	☐
c	☐ x 10 =	50
d	2 x ☐ =	20
e	☐ x 10 =	70
f	3 x 10 =	☐
g	☐ x 10 =	60
h	1 x ☐ =	10

How did you do?

Score.................. Time..................

© Copyright HeadStart Primary Ltd

12

See if you can find all the answers in the time given. Be careful, some of them have been turned around!

1

a	3	x	10	=	☐
b	1	x	10	=	☐
c	6	x	10	=	☐
d	4	x	10	=	☐
e	7	x	10	=	☐
f	2	x	10	=	☐
g	8	x	10	=	☐
h	6	x	10	=	☐

2

a	☐	=	4	x	10
b	☐	=	2	x	10
c	☐	=	5	x	10
d	☐	=	3	x	10
e	☐	=	7	x	10
f	☐	=	6	x	10
g	☐	=	8	x	10
h	☐	=	1	x	10

3

a	☐	x	10	=	80
b	☐	x	10	=	60
c	☐	x	10	=	30
d	☐	x	10	=	50
e	☐	x	10	=	20
f	☐	x	10	=	70
g	☐	x	10	=	10
h	☐	x	10	=	40

4

a	4	x	10	=	☐
b	☐	x	10	=	70
c	☐	=	5	x	10
d	20	=	☐	x	10
e	1	x	☐	=	10
f	☐	=	8	x	10
g	3	x	10	=	☐
h	60	=	☐	x	10

How did you do?

Score.................. Time..................

13

Name ....

You are doing well! Now let's see if you can join the two parts with a line. One has been done for you.

1

a	1 x 10	70
b	2 x 10	40
c	3 x 10	10
d	4 x 10	50
e	5 x 10	20
f	6 x 10	80
g	7 x 10	30
h	8 x 10	60

2

a	2 x 10	60
b	5 x 10	30
c	8 x 10	20
d	3 x 10	40
e	6 x 10	70
f	1 x 10	50
g	4 x 10	10
h	7 x 10	80

3

5 x 10   70   10   7 x 10

80   2 x 10   40   8 x 10   30

3 x 10   60   1 x 10   50

20   4 x 10   6 x 10

How did you do?   Score................. Time.................

14

Spikey's here again! See if you can write the answers on his legs.

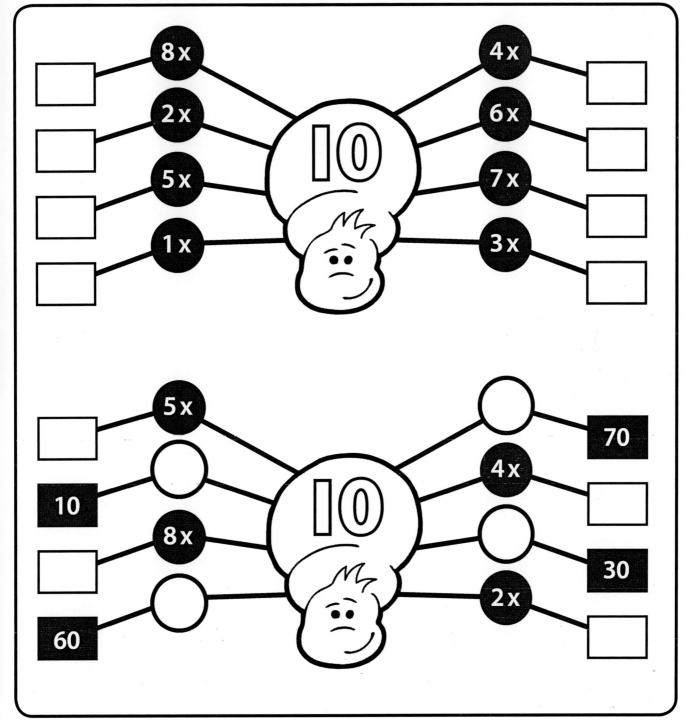

How did you do?

Score................. Time.................

© Copyright HeadStart Primary Ltd

15

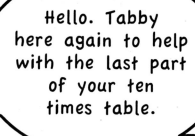

Hello. Tabby here again to help with the last part of your ten times table.

Listen to Tracks 33 and 34 and join in when you are ready.

9 X 10 = 90

 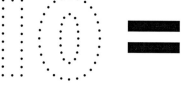 

10 X 10 = 100

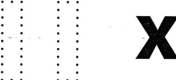  

11 X 10 = 110

12 X 10 = 120

Hi. Can you fill in the spaces with the correct numbers?

1
a 9 x 10 = ☐
b 10 x 10 = ☐
c 11 x 10 = ☐
d 12 x 10 = ☐

2
a 9 x 10 = ☐
b 10 x 10 = ☐
c 11 x 10 = ☐
d 12 x 10 = ☐

3
a ☐ x 10 = 90
b ☐ x 10 = 100
c ☐ x 10 = 110
d ☐ x 10 = 120

4
a ☐ x 10 = 90
b 10 x ☐ = 100
c ☐ x 10 = 110
d 12 x 10 = ☐

How did you do?

Score.................. Time..................

Name ....

( ) minutes!

Now you need to test yourself. See how many you can get right in the time given.

1
a 9 x 10 = ☐
b 10 x 10 = ☐
c 11 x 10 = ☐
d 12 x 10 = ☐
e 11 x 10 = ☐
f 10 x 10 = ☐
g 9 x 10 = ☐
h 12 x 10 = ☐

2
a 12 x 10 = ☐
b 11 x 10 = ☐
c 10 x 10 = ☐
d 9 x 10 = ☐
e 12 x 10 = ☐
f 11 x 10 = ☐
g 10 x 10 = ☐
h 9 x 10 = ☐

3
a 10 x 10 = ☐
b 12 x 10 = ☐
c 11 x 10 = ☐
d 10 x 10 = ☐
e 9 x 10 = ☐
f 11 x 10 = ☐
g 9 x 10 = ☐
h 12 x 10 = ☐

4
a 9 x 10 = ☐
b 11 x 10 = ☐
c 10 x 10 = ☐
d 9 x 10 = ☐
e 12 x 10 = ☐
f 10 x 10 = ☐
g 12 x 10 = ☐
h 11 x 10 = ☐

How did you do?

Score.................. Time..................

© Copyright HeadStart Primary Ltd

18

Draw lines now to join up both parts of the times table. One has been done for you.

1
a 10 x 10 → 110
b 12 x 10 → 90
c 9 x 10 → 100
d 11 x 10 → 120

2
a 11 x 10 → 120
b 10 x 10 → 110
c 12 x 10 → 90
d 9 x 10 → 100

3
120   100
90   110
9 x 10   12 x 10
10 x 10   11 x 10

4
10 x 10   90   11 x 10   12 x 10
110   9 x 10   120   100

How did you do?   ☹

Score................. Time.................

How did you do?   Score.................. Time..................

20

Hello. It's Tabby the Table Dragon here. You are doing really well!

Let's put all the parts together and try to chant the whole ten times table. Listen to Tracks 35 and 36 and join in when you are ready.

Draw over all the numbers with a coloured pencil or felt tip

1 X 10 = 10

2 X 10 = 20

3 X 10 = 30

4 X 10 = 40

5 X 10 = 50

6 X 10 = 60

7 X 10 = 70

8 X 10 = 80

9 X 10 = 90

10 X 10 = 100

11 X 10 = 110

12 X 10 = 120

Name ....

Hello. Try to put the correct answers in the empty boxes. Sets 3 and 4 are on the next page.

1

a	1 x 10 =
b	2 x 10 =
c	3 x 10 =
d	4 x 10 =
e	5 x 10 =
f	6 x 10 =
g	7 x 10 =
h	8 x 10 =
i	9 x 10 =
j	10 x 10 =
k	11 x 10 =
l	12 x 10 =

2

a	12 x 10 =
b	11 x 10 =
c	10 x 10 =
d	9 x 10 =
e	8 x 10 =
f	7 x 10 =
g	6 x 10 =
h	5 x 10 =
i	4 x 10 =
j	3 x 10 =
k	2 x 10 =
l	1 x 10 =

How did you do?

Score.................. Time..................

3

a   3   x   10   =

b   12   x   10   =

c   9   x   10   =

d   6   x   10   =

e   11   x   10   =

f   2   x   10   =

g   8   x   10   =

h   4   x   10   =

i   10   x   10   =

j   5   x   10   =

k   7   x   10   =

l   1   x   10   =

4

a   6   x   10   =

b   ☐   x   10   =   50

c   ☐   x   10   =   110

d   8   x   10   =

e   ☐   x   10   =   120

f   1   x   10   =

g   10   x   10   =

h   ☐   x   10   =   20

i   ☐   x   10   =   90

j   7   x   10   =

k   ☐   x   10   =   40

l   3   x   10   =

Well done; you're doing a great job!

How did you do?

Score.................. Time..................

23

It's race time! Try and beat the clock. See if you can find all the answers in the time given. Try to complete all 4 sets.

[ ] minutes!

1

a	5 x 10 =	[ ]
b	10 x 10 =	[ ]
c	3 x 10 =	[ ]
d	8 x 10 =	[ ]
e	6 x 10 =	[ ]
f	1 x 10 =	[ ]
g	12 x 10 =	[ ]
h	7 x 10 =	[ ]
i	4 x 10 =	[ ]
j	9 x 10 =	[ ]
k	11 x 10 =	[ ]
l	2 x 10 =	[ ]

2

a	[ ] x 10 =	40
b	[ ] x 10 =	120
c	[ ] x 10 =	20
d	[ ] x 10 =	50
e	[ ] x 10 =	110
f	[ ] x 10 =	30
g	[ ] x 10 =	70
h	[ ] x 10 =	90
i	[ ] x 10 =	60
j	[ ] x 10 =	100
k	[ ] x 10 =	80
l	[ ] x 10 =	10

Turn to the next page

3

a ☐ = 10 x 10
b ☐ = 5 x 10
c ☐ = 2 x 10
d ☐ = 12 x 10
e ☐ = 8 x 10
f ☐ = 1 x 10
g ☐ = 11 x 10
h ☐ = 6 x 10
i ☐ = 9 x 10
j ☐ = 4 x 10
k ☐ = 3 x 10
l ☐ = 7 x 10

4

a 12 x 10 = ☐
b 3 x ☐ = 30
c 8 x 10 = ☐
d ☐ x 10 = 50
e ☐ = 11 x 10
f 2 x ☐ = 20
g 9 x 10 = ☐
h ☐ x 10 = 70
i 4 x 10 = ☐
j ☐ = 10 x 10
k 1 x ☐ = 10
l ☐ x 10 = 60

Take care...
some of them
have been
turned around.

How did you do?

Score.................. Time..................

Name ....

You are doing really well! Let's see if you can join the two parts with a line. One has been done for you.

1

a	1 x 10	90
b	2 x 10	50
c	3 x 10	10
d	4 x 10	30
e	5 x 10	120
f	6 x 10	20
g	7 x 10	110
h	8 x 10	40
i	9 x 10	100
j	10 x 10	70
k	11 x 10	80
l	12 x 10	60

2

a	3 x 10	50
b	10 x 10	20
c	6 x 10	120
d	9 x 10	40
e	2 x 10	80
f	11 x 10	60
g	8 x 10	110
h	7 x 10	10
i	5 x 10	100
j	1 x 10	30
k	12 x 10	70
l	4 x 10	90

How did you do?

Score.................. Time..................

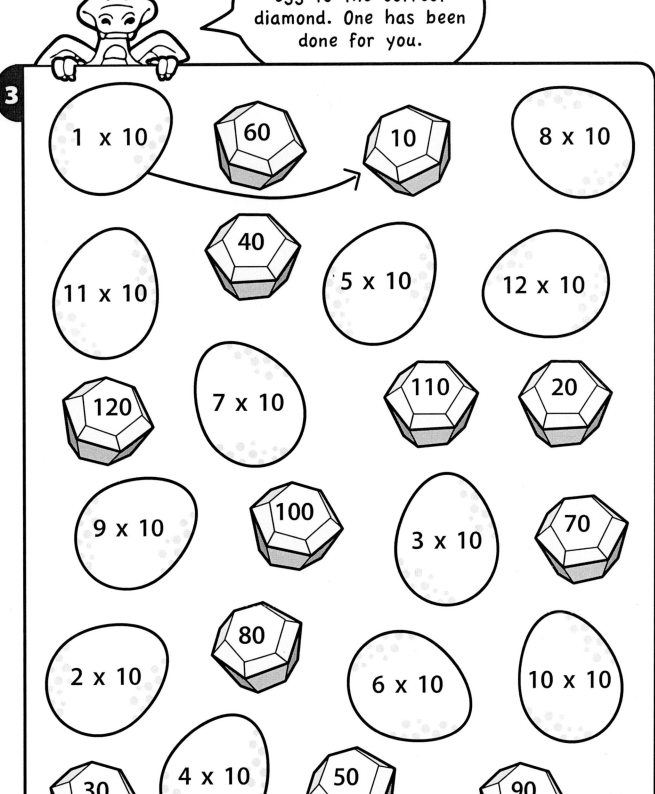

How did you do?   Score.................. Time..................

Name ....

Choose a colour and only fill in the spaces where there is a ten times table answer.

COLOUR BY NUMBERS

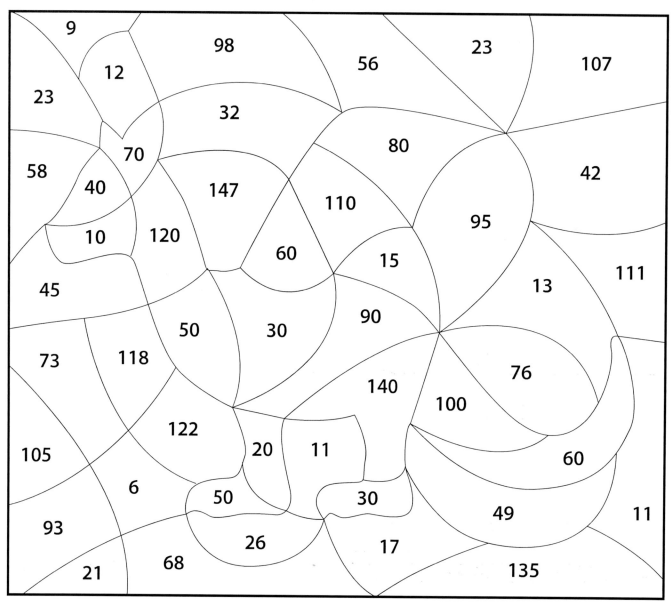

Name ....

MONSTER MONEYBAGS

Dragons love gold! There are 10 gold coins in each purse. How many gold coins would you have if you had...

a 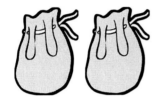   2   x   10   =   ☐

b    ☐   x   10   =   ☐

c 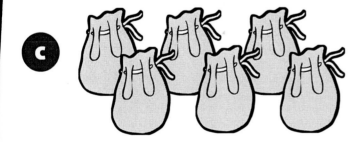   ☐   x   ☐   =   ☐

d    ☐   x   ☐   =   ☐

Can you make up four of your own on a separate piece of paper?

Game time! You need the next page photocopied and at least one other person to play with; also someone to ask the questions.

BINGO!

1. On the blank sheet, write a different answer from the ten times table in each large space. Nine numbers should be written. e.g. 20, 110, etc

2. The person not playing the game randomly chooses questions in the times table. e.g. 'What is three times ten?'

3. If the answer is in a box, it can be crossed out.

4. The first player to cross out all their answers is the winner and must shout, "BINGO!"

5. The caller may wish to give extra rewards for the first person to complete any line or get their four corner numbers.